$1,000 SILVER

WHY SILVER IS POISED TO BE THE
INVESTMENT OF THE CENTURY

B.W. LEETE

ISBN - 9798668632374

for my father
thanks for your two cents

CONTENTS

Author's Note

I am not a financial advisor, broker, dealer, or a provider of professional investment services. The information contained within this book is a mix of fact and my own opinions after 28 years as a numismatist and silver investor. I've also been a stock and Bitcoin trader for several years, at one time studying the markets 40-60 hours a week in addition to my full-time job.

This book is for educational purposes only and the information within should not be taken as expert instruction. Every type of investment has inherent risks, so please do your due diligence before putting any money on the line.

What Is Silver?

Silver is a lustrous transition metal that has the highest reflectivity, thermal conductivity, and electrical conductivity of any metal. On the periodic table of elements silver is represented by the symbol "Ag" and the atomic number 47. Silver is primarily found in the Earth's crust in its pure elemental form, and as an alloy with other metals. Most silver is produced as a byproduct of refining other metals, such as gold, copper, lead, and zinc.

Silver has been valued as a precious metal for thousands of years. As a result, silver has been used in making jewelry, valuable tableware and eating utensils (silverware), and has been used as money in the form of coinage by many civilizations throughout history.

The main focus of this book will be on silver, but silver and gold are inexorably linked in many ways from long before they're removed from the Earth until their final destination in the hands of consumers, jewelry wearers, and precious metals investors. Silver and gold have been considered by some to be the only true money for many centuries and one day they may reclaim that title. Silver and gold were here before the advent of fiat currency, and they'll still be here long after the fiat currency house of cards comes crashing down, as many believe it will.

History of Silver

Coins are believed to have been first introduced as a method of payment sometime between 700 – 600 B.C.[1] The earliest known coins were struck in the kingdom of Lydia in Asia Minor, and were made with electrum, a naturally occurring alloy of silver and gold, that was provided by the river Pactolus.[2] The Lydians minted coins of equal weight in order to make trade smoother and easier. Lydian electrum coins, often bearing the head of a lion, are believed to be the first coins ever minted.

During the reign of King Croesus from 561-546 B.C., silver and gold were refined and used separately in struck coinage.[3]

Athens and Rome began issuing coinage as well, and coin usage flourished in these great civilizations until the Athenian and Roman governments began debasing their coinage. "Debasing" means to reduce in quality or value. The Athenian and Roman governments began to debase their currency by either mixing cheaper metals like copper into their silver and gold coins, or by shaving or clipping small pieces off the coins. The shavings and clippings would eventually be melted down and turned into more currency, devaluing the original coins that were clipped, making them worth less than they were before being altered. The addition of the coinage that was created from the clipped coins further devalues the currency pool.

Currency vs. Money

Currency

Currency can be anything that the ruling powers decree it to be. Currency can be shells, beads, spices, grains, livestock, or printed paper. The island of Yap uses limestone discs (known as "rai") as currency. In an episode of the cartoon *TaleSpin*, bottle caps are used as currency. The episode depicts a wonderful example of hyperinflation when too many bottle caps are dropped from an airplane, devaluing the bottle caps that were already in use. After the vast quantity of bottle caps was dropped, all the caps (both old and new) were then seen as less valuable because of the sheer quantity available. That's precisely how hyperinflation works—but instead of dropping cash from airplanes, more cash is printed and circulated, devaluing the cash already in existence.

As currency typically has no intrinsic value (the paper that a $100 bill is printed on is worth mere pennies), the only value it carries is the value the government sets and that the people believe. Therefore when more of that currency is created and dispersed, the value of all the currency drops in what's known as inflation. The people know more has been created and then they begin to question the value of the currency. If a $100 bill was worth $100 when only a thousand of them were circulating, how can the value remain $100 when there are a million of them circulating? Or a hundred million $100 bills? That's hyperinflation.

Money

Money has intrinsic value. The value is in the item itself, not some arbitrary value placed upon it. Money is durable, transferable, recognizable, can be divided into equal parts, and is found all over the world. Money is also scarce, meaning there is a finite amount. Money is silver and gold.

Silver and gold have been considered money throughout history. The use of paper currency was introduced as claim checks or "I.O.U's" (I owe you) for real money with real intrinsic value so the money itself didn't need to be transported. Initially these claim checks were created to represent the exact quantity of gold in the bank vault. For example, if a bank had $10,000 worth of gold in the vault, then $10,000 worth of claim checks could be issued. With the advent of fractional reserve banking, only a small fraction of the real money was needed to issue claim checks. For instance, if the bank had $10,000 worth of gold in the vault, they were then able to issue claim checks totaling $100,000. This is fractional reserve banking. With currency backed by gold, the bank would only need to keep a fraction of the gold in reserve in order to issue paper claim checks (currency) of many times that amount of gold. Since the exchange of this paper currency became so commonplace and the real money was no longer changing hands as often, governments were able to create an abundance of wealth.

Silver, being the cheaper metal was minted into coins of specific weight. An American silver dollar wasn't worth a dollar because of government decree, a silver dollar was worth a dollar because it contains .77344 of an ounce of silver. An amount that would have been equivalent to a dollar at the time. Silver coinage continued to circulate while gold, being the more valuable metal, was stored in vaults with circulating paper currency merely representing that gold.

The Coinage Act of 1792

The Coinage Act was passed by the United States Congress on April 2, 1792. The act created the U.S. dollar as the country's standard unit of money and established the United States Mint. The Coinage Act also created a decimal system for gold and silver coinage. A gold eagle was worth $10.00 because of the weight of gold it contained. A silver dollar was worth $1.00 because of the weight of the silver it contained. A dime was worth $0.10 because of its silver.

The silver coinage in the United States remained relatively unchanged for nearly two centuries. The design of each coin changed over the years but the amount of silver within remained constant. It wasn't until the 1960's that the price of silver rose enough for the value of the silver in these coins to exceed face value. Meaning the government would lose money with each coin minted because silver prices were higher than the face value of the coin issued.

In the Coinage Act of 1965, signed into law by Lyndon Baines Johnson, the Unites States government debased the currency by minting the same coins with significantly cheaper base metals such as copper and nickel. U.S. dimes and quarters were worth $0.10 and $0.25, respectively, in 1964 because of the silver within. Yet the very next year, the same coins were minted from copper and nickel and continued to hold the same value as the silver coins merely because the government decreed it to be so. U.S. coinage then became fiat currency, meaning the coins themselves no longer had intrinsic value. The value now being only what the government says and the people believe.

Recognizing that the price of silver was higher than the face value of silver coins minted in 1964 and the years prior, people began pulling these silver coins from circulation and hoarding them. The silver in John F. Kennedy half dollars was reduced from 90% of the coin's weight to 40% of the coin's weight, effectively eliminating over half the value of the coin while the face value remained the same. JFK half dollars were 40% silver from 1965 to 1970 and then the silver was removed entirely.

Even United States copper coinage wasn't safe from currency debasement. In the United States, small cents were minted out of copper from 1856 – 1982. When the price of copper exceeded the face value of small cents, the government replaced the copper with zinc, a far cheaper metal. U.S. small cents from 1982 onward have contained a zinc core with a plating of copper so they still look like a penny. U.S. cents after 1982 look the same and spend the same as they always have, only now they contain only $1/10^{th}$ of the amount of copper they had for more than a century. Copper is not a precious metal, but it's an incredibly useful metal. The value of small cents was originally due to the amount of copper they were minted from, but not anymore. Today the intrinsic value of all coinage is gone. These coins continue to carry value simply because the public believes they do and spends them the same as they always have.

With the copper missing from pennies, the silver missing from silver coinage, and the paper currency no longer backed by gold, the entire world now runs on fiat currency—currency that has value only because "they" say so and we believe them.

Free Market

For nearly 100 years, the price of gold was set at a mostly fixed rate between $18.93 and $20.67. In 1934 the U.S. Gold Reserve Act was signed into law by President Franklin Delano Roosevelt. The act outlawed most private gold ownership, forcing citizens to sell their gold back to the U.S. Treasury. The Gold Reserve Act also increased the fixed price of gold from $20.67 to $35 an ounce, where it remained until 1971 when President Richard Nixon removed all ties between the U.S. dollar and gold. With the dollar no longer tied to gold, gold entered the free market and prices began to rise. By December 31, 1974 when President Gerald Ford signed a bill legalizing private gold ownership once again, the price had risen from $35 to over $100 on the open market. In three years the price of gold had tripled.

In early 1975 the price of gold was around $150 an ounce. By January 1980, investors had bid the price of gold up to $850 an ounce. In less than 10 years, the price of gold increased from $35 to $850. That's a 2,400% increase. Never before in history had the value of gold seen such a tremendous rise. Behold! the power of the free market.

Silver made a similar move in the same timeframe, increasing from a high of $1.75 in 1971 to a high of $49.45 in 1980. The Hunt Brothers (Nelson Bunker Hunt, William Herbert Hunt, and Lamar Hunt) had attempted to corner the silver market, but who's to say how much of the rise in silver prices was directly attributable to them? The rise in silver prices in more recently years is entirely unrelated to the Hunt Brothers. So what is driving the price of silver and gold these days? There are innumerable factors, but suffice it to say that silver and gold trade on the free market, so they are always seeking fair market value.

$50 Silver

The price of silver hit $50 (almost) in 1980 and then began to sell off. Seeking fair market value the price of silver had gone too high, too fast, and then began to descend. The price bounced up and down between $5 and $20 for a few years before finally settling around $5 in 1986. The price of silver and gold languished for nearly 20 years before they began to rise once more around 2003-2005.

Economic factors drove investors back to silver and on April 25, 2011, the price of silver reached $49.80. Silver has been experiencing a selloff in the years since 2011, with the price per ounce being around $15.20 as I write this paragraph. The price of silver is now but a fraction of what it was in 1980 and 2011. Can you think of *anything* else that is currently about 1/3 of the price it was 40 years ago? The current silver price has been languishing around $15, roughly the same as silver's 1983 high of $14.67. Silver is currently cheaper than it was for most of 2008 and 2009, more than a decade ago. The price of virtually everything else save for *Betamax* has appreciated over the years while silver has remained the same or has even decreased over time. Even gold has a much stronger 40 year chart than silver, as gold has mostly held its gains. Why is the price of silver faltering? Why is this particular asset so strongly undervalued? Many investors (often called "silver bugs" or "silver stackers") believe silver will hit $50 again one day, but could it reach new highs?

The value of assets tends to cycle back and forth between overvalued and undervalued. It so happens that in the last few years, silver has been significantly undervalued. When an asset is undervalued, the masses tend to shy away from that asset, often while the more informed and experienced investors are buying. It's the old stock market adage: buy the fear, sell the greed. Meaning when silver hit $49, many of the investors who'd amassed their silver stacks at $5-15 dollars an ounce were selling and getting out, knowing that such skyrocketing prices wouldn't last forever. Then when silver prices are languishing as they did throughout the 1990's, and as they are currently, the experienced investors are loading up for yet another run up to $49. They know that these things happen in waves and cycles.

All we would need for silver to reach $49 once more is for a portion of the public to recognize that silver is currently undervalued and to start buying again. Silver prices can be highly volatile, and in theory it wouldn't take much more than a nudge to send the precious metal back to its 2011 highs. The price of silver has already reached $49 twice, it would not seem unreasonable to most investors to suggest that it could happen again soon.

Many investors believe that the real *value* of silver has already reached and surpassed $50 per ounce, and that the *price* of silver is determined by the paper price. Meaning that silver derivatives dictate the price of silver, keeping the actual price of physical silver artificially low. We'll cover that more in depth later on.

$100 Silver

Silver/Gold Ratio

Throughout most of history, gold and silver were seen as money and they circulated as such. The price of gold was generally about 12 times the price of silver, as silver was more abundant than gold by a factor of 12. Therefore 1 ounce of gold would have the same value as 12 ounces of silver. Due to the relative rarity between these two metals remaining constant, this 12 to 1 ratio held true for thousands of years. The United States Coinage Act of 1792 also had nearly the same ratio at approximately 15 ounces of silver to 1 ounce of gold.

It wasn't until the late 19th century when large silver discoveries and other factors caused the silver/gold price ratio to widen, eventually bringing the value of 1 ounce of gold to equal that of approximately 100 ounces of silver. Consider that for a moment. For thousands of years, the amount of silver from mining production was roughly 12 ounces of silver for every 1 ounce of gold mined. Therefore what makes gold more valuable isn't necessarily its attractiveness to the eye, it's the relative scarcity between the two metals. When silver discoveries and mining advances vastly increased the quantities of above-ground available silver, the ratio widened tremendously and silver became much cheaper than gold at a ratio of 100 to 1.

A century later the silver/gold ratio finally reverted back to its original ratio (roughly) when gold reached $850 an ounce in 1980 and silver hit $50. That's a ratio of 17 to 1, putting the silver gold price ratio right back to where it began. The silver/gold price ratio oscillates over time, swinging back and forth from overvalued to undervalued. The ratio widened again and for much of the 1990's it was around 60-70 to 1. Then in 2011 the ratio began reverting back toward that 12 to 1. Silver hit a high of $49 in April 2011 and gold followed in

August 2011 with a high of $1,917. Silver reached its peak a few months before gold. When silver hit $49 that year, the price of gold was hovering around $1,500 an ounce. That gives us a ratio of 30 to 1. The silver/gold price ratio was trying to revert back to its historical number but never quite made it. Then the price of silver began to falter while gold continued to climb higher, further widening the gap.

The price of silver at this moment as I write in March 2019 is $15.19 and the price of gold is $1,295.96. That puts the current silver to gold ratio at 85.32 to 1. So we can begin to see the clear swings of the pendulum that is the silver/gold price ratio. Began at 12 to 1, widened to 100 to 1, then it narrowed once more back to 17 to 1, then it swung back the other way to 60 or 70 to 1 throughout the 1990's, then it began to narrow once again and reached about 30 to 1, and finally here we stand currently at 85 to 1. At 85 to 1 this is the widest the silver/gold price ratio has been in the last three decades.

Eventually the silver/gold price ratio will swing the other direction and the spread will begin to narrow again. The spread hasn't reached near to the historical 12 to 1 ratio in nearly 40 years. We're due for a revisit to those numbers.

Let's pretend for a moment that there are no other factors at play to influence the price of silver. Let's say all that matters is the silver/gold price ratio and the swinging of the pendulum that carries the spread from wide to narrow and back again. With the current gold price of $1,295.96, if we apply the 30 to

1 ratio that was reached in 2011, the current price of silver would be about $43.

Let's apply the 17 to 1 ratio that was reached in 1980. That would bring the price of silver to around $76. With that price we've reached uncharted territory for silver, with $76 being significantly higher than it has ever been. $76 dollar silver is about five times greater than where the price is currently. It may seem nearly impossible for the price of silver to climb that high, but let's consider that $49 silver is more than three times higher than where the price sits as I'm writing this. If $49 isn't too ridiculous, neither is $76.

Now let's say that the price ratio reverts back to its historical norm. If gold remains at $1,295.96, the ratio of 12 to 1 would put the price of silver at $108. If we stretch our imaginations a bit and suppose that gold returns to its all time high of $1,900. With gold at its all time high, a price ratio of 12 to 1 would bring the price of silver to $158. These numbers are very plausible. The ratio is due to return to 12 to 1 eventually. It was there for thousands of years and has revisited (or nearly revisited) a few times since. Gold has already reached $1,900. These things have already occurred, but they haven't yet occurred at the same time. What is stopping these factors from lining up again so that the price of silver meets or exceeds $100? Does it really seem that far-fetched?

$671 Silver

Earlier we went over the fact that the U.S. dollar is no longer backed by gold. In fact, there are no nations left in the world that still back their currency with gold. All the currency of the world is now backed by absolutely nothing but the government's word that a dollar is worth a dollar. Our money no longer contains silver. Silver and gold had been money for thousands of years and now they practically have nothing to do with money. Money is printed paper and numbers on a computer screen. Even the words "print more money" hardly make sense anymore as most of the money isn't printed, it's merely figures on a screen that are manipulated at will by the Federal Reserve.

While money is no longer backed by gold and no longer contains silver, the values of silver and gold are still measured by the dollar. The *prices* of silver and gold only seem to have risen over the years, when in fact it's the *value* of the dollar that is diminishing. For example, a 1960 U.S. Washington quarter would have purchased a gallon of gasoline in 1960. In 2019, nearly 60 years later, the silver weight of that exact same 1960 Washington quarter is worth $2.73. Local gas prices are currently hovering around $2.39. That quarter is still more than enough to buy a gallon of gas. All you have to do is take that quarter into almost any coin shop or antique shop and they'll give you about 90% of the silver weight, or about $2.46.

The quarter has retained its value after all these years because silver has retained its value. The dollar, on the other hand, has not. Today the dollar retains approximately 14% of the purchasing power it had in 1960. The reason for this precipitous drop in purchasing power of the dollar is because of the immense pool of dollars that exists today compared to the dollars that existed in 1960. Remembering that episode of *TaleSpin* when the airplane dropped vast quantities of bottle caps (currency), the bottle caps that were already being used as a medium of exchange were devalued. It's called hyperinflation and it's exactly what happened in Weimar Germany in the early 1920's, and in Zimbabwe in the early 2000's. The United States has not yet reached the point of *hyper*-inflation, but inflation has taken its toll over the decades, devaluing the dollar immensely since 1913.[4]

Prominent precious metals dealer and collector Michael Maloney believes that the price of silver and gold will periodically rise to meet or exceed the total number of dollars in existence. He claims that silver and gold, always seeking fair market value, will eventually rise to account for the entire currency supply. UsDebtClock.org estimates that the current dollar to silver ratio is $671 per ounce. If Michael Maloney's theory is true, and the prices of silver and gold will eventually rise to match or exceed the currency supply, it means the price of silver will rise to $671 per ounce. In theory, that could indeed be the current *value* of silver measured against the dollar, while multiple factors are keeping the *price* of silver artificially low.

If the only two factors we were to focus on here are the silver/gold ratio and the currency supply measured against the amount of above-ground available silver, it wouldn't be unreasonable to suggest that one day in the not-too-distant future, the price of silver may rise to account for the currency supply, causing $671 silver. However, there are many factors at play that make silver scarce, important, and uniquely in demand. Silver is one of the most undervalued assets, and it's quite possible that silver may one day prove itself to be the greatest investment opportunity of all time.

$1,000 Silver

What Makes Silver Unique?

There are many factors that make $671 silver seem low. Silver is an especially unique and useful metal, and we're currently in a period of history in which the demand for silver has never been higher. Many different factors have aligned just right to suggest that we've been heading into a perfect storm that could catapult the prices of silver far higher than the world has seen or can imagine.

To begin with, silver is far more useful than gold. Gold has few actual uses. Gold is collected and hoarded in bullion form as a store of value, gold is used in dentistry, it is used to make jewelry and gold leaf, and it is used in electronics in small quantities. Gold is the most malleable of all metals, often only a minute amount is required, with some sources stating that less than 0.034 grams of gold are used to produce a typical cell phone.[5]

Silver has the highest thermal and electrical conductivity of all metals, making it one of the most useful metals for use in electronics. Silver's price in comparison to gold, and it's greater thermal and electrical conductivity makes it the desired metal for industrial use.

Silver has a multitude of industrial uses that cannot be replaced by any other metal. Silver is used in mirrors and reflective coatings, soldering, photography, solar panels, water purification, batteries, cell phones, laptops and other electronics, CD's, DVD's, electrical conductors, ball bearings, LED's and RFID chips. This is a partial list. Silver has hundreds of industrial uses. Here's the thing most people don't know and don't care about: most of the silver that is used in these applications is used in such small amounts, the silver cannot be reclaimed. In many cases it is burned up, used, gone for good. In other cases the silver *can* be reclaimed, but it's not always cost-effective to remove minute amounts of silver from certain things. Silver consumed in such a way cannot be reclaimed or recycled and once it is used it is gone for good.

Silver is known primarily as a precious metal. People are familiar with silver jewelry, silverware, and perhaps silver dollars. The general public doesn't know about silver's unique demand as one of the most useful metals. They don't know that silver is a consumable commodity that is being used, burned up, thrown away. Of the various uses of silver, only a few result in the metal being saved. Silver is truly a vanishing resource.

Industrial demand for silver has never been higher, and it continues to grow.[6] Industry has been the biggest net buyer of silver for decades. With the advent of consumer electronics over the last half-century, the demand for silver has grown as the demand for consumer electronics has grown. Some sources estimate that in 1950, there were around 10 billion ounces of above-ground available silver, whereas by 1980, the quantity was down to approximately 3-4 billion ounces of above-ground available silver.[7]

More silver is mined every year, but most silver comes as a by-product of mining other metals, such as gold, copper, and zinc. It's difficult for miners to mine more silver to keep up with demand because primary silver producers are rare. The low cost of silver over the years also proves as a hindrance to mining efforts, as it's often cost prohibitive to mine for silver exclusively. In other words, industry needs to wait for the gold and copper miners to provide their silver, and silver is merely a fraction of the business of the gold and copper miners. When the price of silver rises, more primary silver producers will appear and silver mining efforts will ramp up, but even then silver is a finite resource. How much is left in the Earth's crust? The United States Geological Survey has estimated that there is less silver left in the Earth than any other metal.[8] If industrial silver demand continues to grow and production rates continue, the USGS has stated that all silver reserves will eventually be exhausted.

Once remaining silver deposits in the Earth's crust become depleted, industry will turn elsewhere to get the silver it needs. It will turn to anywhere it can get silver and it will pay whatever it must to get it.

Why Are Silver Prices So Low?

Silver currently has the highest demand it's ever had in history. According to the laws of supply and demand, when the demand is high and the available supply is low, the price of that consumer commodity will rise. So what's going on with the laws of supply and demand, why are silver prices not rising to absurdly high levels? Why are people not rioting in the streets, knocking each other over to get to the coins shops to buy silver?

The answer lies in the silver derivatives market. Often referred to as "paper silver" silver derivatives are things that trade in place of real, physical silver. Futures contracts and Exchange Traded Funds are examples of silver derivatives.

When a commodities investor wants to trade or invest in silver or gold, he or she may buy a futures contract in lieu of purchasing a wheelbarrow full of physical metal. In the same vein as Fractional Reserve Banking, where only one $20 gold coin would need to be held in a bank's vault for the bank to issue up to $100 of cash, silver derivatives trade at many times the amount of physical silver that exists. Some sources claim that the futures market for silver is upwards of 500 times greater than the amount of physical silver that exists in the world.[9] With the "paper silver" market being so much larger than the physical silver market, the paper silver market dictates the price of silver.

The price of silver is being set based on tremendous amounts of silver that doesn't even exist! The demand is high, but so is the supply. The problem being that the supply is imaginary. The true supply is dwindling but the public doesn't know because the paper silver market controls everything. Additionally, there are a few "large entities" that are believed to hold enormous short positions in silver. A short position is when an investor believes the price of a security or commodity will go *down*, so they "sell it short" by betting against it. It's the opposite of "going long" which is when an investor buys the security or commodity with the anticipation that the price will *rise*. A large entity with deep pockets could theoretically sell large enough short positions to keep the price of a security or commodity artificially low. There is absolutely no other commodity with active short positions as large as those believed to be held in silver.[10]

Why would they want to do this? One reason is because the entity also wants to invest by going long. They'll suppress the price of silver on one hand via the paper markets, and then on the other hand they'll buy physical silver at absurdly low prices because they know the price will eventually rise no matter what. Another reason an entity might want to keep the price of silver low is so the public won't catch on about how high the value truly is. For example, if gold were to reach the price of $10,000 per ounce, people might begin to catch on that it's not the price of gold that is rising, but the value of the U.S. dollar that is falling. For fiat currency to continue working there has to be a delicate balance. People need to believe that cash is king and gold and silver are just pretty jewelry metals with no other practical uses. The big boys want to keep the wealth in the hands of the big boys…not the general public.

A small percentage of the general public seems to be aware of silver's usefulness and rarity. If more investors begin to catch on to what's happening with silver prices, they will flock to silver, driving demand much higher. One day the silver price manipulation could fail, as large numbers of people flock to silver, and silver short sellers could get squeezed as silver prices take off.

It's not unrealistic to think that one day the price of silver could reach $1,000 per ounce. The price of gold was less than $20 per ounce for many years, then it rose to the $30 to $35 range, where it stayed for many years. Then within eight years, gold went from the $40 range to $850, an increase of more than 2,100%. Gold made a similar move from a low of around $250 in 2000 to over $1,000 in 2009. In 2011 gold hit $1,917, a 760% increase from its low in 2000. If silver were to make a similar move, a 760% increase from $15.19 would put the silver price at $115 per ounce. If silver were to increase 2,100% from current levels as gold did from 1972 to 1980, that would put the silver price at about $320. All factors considered, this could be a low estimate. The potential for the price of silver to increase is astronomical.

$10,000 Silver?

In his book *$10,000 Gold: Why Gold's Inevitable Rise Is the Investor's Safe Haven*, Nick Barisheff makes an excellent case for how the price of gold could reach such lofty highs. Multiple economic factors could push the gold price to $10,000, but what about silver? If above-ground available silver is more rare than above-ground available gold, and silver has many times the usefulness and demand of gold, there's nothing to stop the price of silver from continuing to rise to meet and even exceed the historic 12 to 1 ratio of silver and gold prices. If silver continues to be consumed and the public catches on to what a rare and unique investment opportunity silver has become, there's nothing to stop the price of silver to rise to equal or even exceed the price of gold.

Silver prices are much more volatile than gold prices. Silver prices are low right now but that could change quickly. A move back to $49 silver would not be difficult and could feasibly come quickly. In the event of an economic crisis, investors turn to physical assets, things that tend to retain their value, such as commodities, land, silver and gold. With gold currently around $1,300 per ounce, gold looks expensive to many investors. If the price of gold were to rise a few hundred dollars from current levels, it will look even more expensive. With gold becoming too expensive, people will begin to realize that silver is still affordable and silver has the unique potential. As investors flock to silver, industry will be trying to buy up all they can knowing the prices are on the rise, all while stockpiles are dwindling and mining efforts continue to yield diminishing returns. That's when the general public will become aware that the world is literally running out of silver. When this happens, the price of silver could not only match the price of gold, but it could rocket past gold, so that in theory, one day the price of silver could feasibly be many times the price of gold.

In his book $10,000 Gold, Nick Barisheff estimates that two billion ounces of gold exist in bullion form, whereas the entire world silver supply is currently around one billion ounces.[11] If these numbers are correct, silver is already rarer than gold and continues to grow even more rare as time passes. With silver being both more rare and more useful than gold, both of these metals will eventually find their fair market value. With industrial demand for silver continuing to rise, fair market value for these metals could eventually turn out to be something like $10,000 gold and $100,000 silver. After more than 30 years experience in the financial industry, Bix Weir has called $100,000 silver a "conservative estimate" and gives twenty reasons why that price could happen in an article he wrote on *The Road to Roota*. A silver price of $100,000 per ounce may seem outrageously absurd compared to the $15 and change price of the metal today, but if the demand is high enough and the supply is low enough, it's definitely within the realm of possibility.

If the time comes when industrial demand and investor demand both surge simultaneously while the silver supply continues to dwindle to record lows, there's no telling how high the price of silver could go. If we then add in the fact the currency supply is massively greater than it has ever been and all of it is free-floating fiat currency backed by nothing, that gives us a perfect storm that could prove to be the greatest financial shift the world has seen in modern times.

Silver doesn't need a currency crisis in order for the metal to find its true market value. The case for silver is unique enough that the house of cards that is fiat currency could theoretically continue onward as it has for the last hundred years and all the other factors relating to silver could rocket the price to $1,000 or higher. Silver is one of the most undervalued investments of all time. The increasing demand and dwindling supply could be enough to ignite silver prices once investors realize its worth and begin rushing in. For anyone not interested in silver or gold because they believe that the U.S. dollar will hold strong, they're right. In theory it's possible that the dollar will never crash and a currency crisis will never happen. Those people will still miss out if and when silver proves it doesn't need a currency crisis to reach its potential.

On the other hand, if a currency crisis *does* occur, it will push the price of silver that much higher. In the event of a currency crisis, if inflation or hyperinflation has smashed the value of the U.S. dollar, the general public's confidence in currency will fail. In the German hyperinflation, the value of the papiermark fell so rapidly, people were scrambling to put their money into *anything* that would hold its value. Have you ever heard the story of the woman who was pushing a wheelbarrow full of papiermarks down the street to buy a loaf of bread when someone came along, took the wheelbarrow from her, dumped out all the worthless currency and ran away with the wheelbarrow? In times of a currency crisis such as the hyperinflation that plagued Weimar Germany, people turn to anything that retains its value, such as food, land, real estate, silver, gold, and wheelbarrows.

How High?

How high will silver prices climb? It's impossible to say for sure, but $50 an ounce is a good starting point, considering the price of the metal has already reached that height twice in recent times. A doubling in price from $50 to $100 would not be difficult and could feasibly happen in a year or two, or even less time, depending on how rapidly the demand increases. From $100 the price of silver will most likely climb higher until it eventually reaches $500 and then $1,000. This may take several years, with the price of silver fluctuating in the meantime. Prices rarely go straight up, they rise a bit, then they dip. After the dip, prices begin to rise again, maybe then they trade sideways for a while before beginning the climb back up again. Rarely does the price of any security or commodity go straight up without entering a correction period during which the price drops and languishes. We're in a long-term price correction right now. After silver reached $49 in 2011 and gold hit $1,900 they've both been in a price correction in the years since. Silver took a few years to fall to a low of around $13.90 and gold fell to $1,050 before the metals began climbing again. In the years since that low, gold has performed better than silver, widening the silver/gold price ratio and making silver seem immensely unloved and undervalued. This makes for an excellent opportunity for those who are able to see what's happening.

It's hard to say whether the price of silver will ever reach $10,000 or the $100,000 "conservative estimate" given by Bix Weir, but $1,000 silver seems realistic, especially when we take into account that gold has already made similar price moves. If gold can do it, why can't silver?

One thing we must keep in mind when attempting to speculate on how high the price of silver could rise is that we're measuring the price of silver against the U.S. dollar. The price of silver measured against the price of gold is currently 85 ounces of silver to 1 ounce of gold. If the price ratio were to narrow and the price of silver rose faster than the price of gold, then let's say the ratio reaches 15 ounces of silver for 1 ounce of gold. At that ratio, we know the price of silver is rising strongly relative to the price of gold. Now let's say that the price of silver measured against the U.S. dollar is currently 15 dollars to one ounce of silver, but then the dollar/silver price ratio widens to 85 dollars to 1 ounce of silver. There are many ways to measure the value of silver, measuring it against the dollar is only one way.

Throughout history, the value of fiat currencies always revert to zero, during which there is a period of hyperinflation. If the U.S. dollar were to enter a period of hyperinflation, it's feasible the dollar could be rendered utterly worthless in much the same way the only value in a wheelbarrow full of German papiermarks was the value of the wheelbarrow itself. At the height of the hyperinflation of the Weimar Republic in 1923, a loaf of bread cost upward of 200 billion marks.[12] In theory, a similar currency crisis in the United States could put a price tag on silver greater than $1 trillion dollars per ounce. In the case that we've reached the point of $1 trillion dollars per 1 ounce of silver, it would be pointless to continue measuring the price of silver against the dollar. With such extreme hyperinflation, it would make more sense to measure the value of silver against the value of dirt. At least the dirt will retain its usefulness.

In his book *Guide to Investing in Gold and Silver*, Michael Maloney states that at the height of German hyperinflation, an entire city block of commercial real estate in downtown Berlin could be purchased for a mere 25 ounces of gold, worth about $500 U.S. dollars at that time. During the hyperinflation of the Weimar Republic, those who had silver and gold had true wealth and those who relied on currency faced dark times.

The question "How high will silver prices go?" is therefore difficult to answer. The safest answer is that silver will eventually find it's fair market value.

When?

When will this all happen? That's the best question of all. Unfortunately no one knows the answer. Economists and precious metals enthusiasts are shocked that it isn't already happening. Maybe it is happening, only slower than expected. Many factors have kept the value of currency afloat and the prices of precious metals suppressed. With the Dow Jones Industrial Average currently at $25,849 the general public has retained its confidence in the stock market and other paper assets, the U.S. dollar included. The economy shows signs of improvements and things are looking good. The stock market shows strong signs of being in a bubble. Many believe we were headed for a market crash in 2015, which was staved off with the election of Trump and his efforts to boost the economy. Many also believe that the stock market is being propped up artificially, and that the factors at play leading to a stock market crash and a currency crisis have been abated only for the time being.

If we are indeed headed into a market crash, such an event could theoretically kick off a large-scale currency crisis and catapult the United States (or possibly the whole world) into another Great Depression. If this were to happen, it's believed that wealth would transfer from those who hold currency and other paper assets—to those who hold real assets and real money.

In trying to determine *when* this will happen, we must also take into account the unique factors for silver itself. Let's say that the value of both the stock market and the U.S. dollar stays artificially propped up for another decade. With the dollar remaining strong, and the stock marking holding around the $25,000 to $30,000 range for another ten years, that gives us plenty of time to watch the silver supply dwindle. In that time, mining efforts could also slow to a crawl as the silver in the Earth's crust is being depleted. In such a scenario, a currency crisis wouldn't be necessary to send the price of silver soaring. Increased industrial demand and increased investor demand, in conjunction with an ever-dwindling silver supply is enough to send the precious metal to $50, $100, even $1,000 or more per ounce.

In 2011 many believed we were already headed in that direction. Perhaps we still are. Perhaps the sell-off in precious metals since 2012 and 2013 has been nothing more than a temporary dip in the rising prices. Once again, rarely does the price or value of a security or commodity go straight up without taking dips and moving sideways for a period of time, confusing investors. With silver prices floundering under $20 for so long, it's amazing more investors haven't recognized what a tremendous opportunity exists. The last time precious metals were beaten down to such a degree was in the 1990's— right before the prices of both precious metals began to take off.

During the period from 1991 to 2001 when the Dow Jones Industrial Average rose from around $2,700 to $10,700 per share, silver and gold were unloved. Precious metals were then in a period of history when they were perhaps the *most* unloved. Many investors got burned buying silver in the $40-50 range and gold in the $750-850 range and therefore considered the two metals to be all but worthless in the 1990's. The general public was done with silver and gold. At a time when 99% of investors were focused on the bull run of the stock market, no one was paying attention to silver and gold. Or so it seemed. On the contrary, smart investors know to buy the weakness and sell the strength. When the general public considered silver and gold to be worthless, the smart investors were buying.

Smart investors who bought silver in the 1990's then began to sell their silver as the public was slowly catching on around the $20 per ounce mark. Many investors who bought their silver between $4 and $6 were happy to cash out at $20 or $25, selling to new investors who were just getting on board. Little did many of those smart investors know what silver would reach $49 before the bull run began to subside. The *smartest* investors likely sold around the $40-49 range and then began to load up again once prices dipped under $20 per ounce. The general public always chases old news, and now as people continue to pile into the stock market, the smartest investors are loading up on silver at these insanely cheap prices under $20. Once the public begins to catch on, $15 to $20 silver will be in the past, trailing behind in the rearview mirror, perhaps never to be seen again.

The smartest investors are buying silver right now. Some have never stopped buying silver. They know what the general public doesn't know—that silver is unloved, undervalued, and has the potential to be one of the biggest investment opportunities of the century. They know industry is buying silver in mass quantities. They know much of that silver purchased by industry will be consumed, used, burned up and never reclaimed. They know what a unique opportunity exists in silver. They know that when something so valuable and so useful is so ridiculously undervalued, that it will only be a matter of time before the public realizes it and silver prices take off. Then many of those smart investors will be selling their silver for a handsome profit...while the smartest investors won't be selling. They know $50 silver is peanuts. They're waiting for the big moves they know are coming. Many have been preparing for it for decades.

Between the end of 2008 and the beginning of 2011, the price of silver rose from $10 per ounce to $49 per ounce. Many investors recognized this as a bubble, gains that could not be sustained despite the fact that the fundamentals were in place. Many of those investors sold for a hefty profit and then waited for a dip to buy back in. They got more than a dip, the price of silver tanked from $49 to $13.90 in a little more than four years. It took about two years to rise and then twice the length of time to fall. Few investors could have been able to anticipate the precipitous fall from $49 to $13.90, but many saw that as a blessing. They know the fundamentals for silver are unique and strong, with many investors seeing the price drop as nothing more than a wonderful buying opportunity. They know nothing has changed for silver, and the longer the price stays at these lows levels, the stronger silver will bounce back when the time comes. Once again, while the silver price flounders at these low levels under $20, most investors and the public think silver is done. Many probably bought at levels above $30 and got burned selling at below $20. Now they're reluctant to ever touch silver again. They sold their silver cheaply to the smart investors who have never stopped buying because their vision is a little bit clearer and they can see the perfect storm coming on the horizon.

So when will this happen? If the United States Geological Survey is accurate in their estimates for how much silver remains in the Earth's crust, we could begin to see some major silver shortages within the next 5-10 years. Industrial demand for silver is higher than mining production. If industrial demand continues to grow and the supply continues to diminish, we should begin to see some major price moves and new highs within the next 5 years. This also depends on how long the "big boys" are able to keep the price of silver artificially low. Remember the current *value* of silver could well be higher than $50 to $100 per ounce already. Also, silver is much more volatile than gold and moves more quickly. The price of silver could theoretically rise from the $15 range to $50 in a matter of months or even weeks. If the perfect storm were to hit silver, the price could feasibly reach $1,000 in a short period of time. There's little precedent because silver is such a unique metal with unique potential, so it's a matter of speculation, but the dominoes are all lined up, waiting for that initial flick.

What Are Your Goals?

The first question you'll want to ask yourself is are you looking to *trade* silver, or are you looking to *invest* for the long-term? You can always do both, as many investors do. Often investing will teach you tricks or habits that may help you to successfully trade silver, and trading silver can teach you tricks and habits that will help you when investing in silver. It all depends on what your goals are.

Are you looking to add some precious metals to your investment portfolio, or are you a silver bug looking to acquire as much as you can for the coming rise in precious metals prices? Are you looking to trade the volatility in price fluctuations, or are you interested in investing for the long-term? Do you see the opportunity in silver as a means of earning lots of currency in the future when you sell, or do you see silver and gold as the real money and you want to collect as much as possible?

It may be helpful to write down your goals and take time to consider what it will take to reach them. If you're interested in making as much money (er, currency) as possible in a short time, trading is your best bet. On a day to day basis, neither silver nor gold have enough volatility to make it worthwhile to buy and sell physical metal frequently. This is why silver and gold derivatives were created. If you're looking to invest for the long haul, you'll want to collect physical metal. If you're looking to trade with the intention of making short-term profits in currency that you'll then turn around and use to purchase physical metal as an investment, it will be helpful for you to research not only precious metals investment, but also commodities trading, futures contracts, options, Exchange Traded Funds (ETFs), mining companies, and even the stock market. The broader your spectrum of knowledge on all these topics, the easier it will be to trade and invest in precious metals successfully.

Trading Silver

Mining Companies

If you're looking to trade silver but you want to keep your risk minimal, trading silver mining companies is a good way to go. Stocks in mining companies trade the same as stocks in any other publicly traded company. To trade stocks in silver mining companies, you'll need a broker. Whether you're using an old-school broker, or an online brokerage like E-Trade or TD Ameritrade, you're in charge of deciding how much to buy, when to buy, and when to sell.

Trading mining companies is the easiest route, as Exchange Traded Funds, futures contracts, and options can be difficult to understand if you're a beginner. Trading stock in mining companies requires no margin or leverage (unless you're shorting) and you can begin with a limited supply of funds, often whatever the minimum is to open an account with the brokerage. When using an online brokerage, you're in complete control of every aspect of the trade from beginning to end. The only thing you're not in control of is the price action of the mining stocks.

Trading stock in mining companies is the best and safest option for beginners. There are only a few main drawbacks. The first drawback being that if you don't keep watch of the shares you own, you could feasibly lose a lot of money. This is why you'll want to keep a close eye on your positions and sell when (or before) your loss becomes too great. The other biggest drawback is that stocks in mining companies are often not very volatile and don't fluctuate much from day to day, so you may not yield much in profits on your successful trades.

On a positive note, there are quite a few mining companies to chose from, each of them being unique and having their own characteristics and degrees of success. Here's a select list of only a few mining companies and their ticker symbols:

- Pan American Silver Corp. (PAAS)
- First Majestic Silver Corp. (AG)
- Coeur Mining (CDE)
- Great Panther Silver Ltd. (GPL)
- MAG Silver Corp. (MAG)
- Hecla Mining (HL)
- Endeavor Silver Corp. (EXK)
- Fortuna Silver Mines Inc. (FSM)

You'll want to do some research to understand how these mining companies work and to determine which ones will be most suitable for you and your trading needs and parameters. Comparing fluctuations in both spot silver prices and the share price of mining companies can help you understand the correlation between the two and how these mining companies are affected by changes in spot silver price.

Exchange Traded Funds

ETFs are one example of silver derivatives. ETFs are a form of paper that trades in place of physical gold or physical silver. ETFs are part of why the paper silver market dwarfs the physical silver market, and thus, dictates the price of silver.

If you're looking to *invest* in silver, silver ETFs are not the way. However, if you're looking to *trade* silver, ETFs are an excellent option. They trade the same as stocks and are relatively easy for a beginner to learn and trade.

There are ETFs that are not leveraged and their price action is similar to that of spot silver. If silver goes up 5% on the day, silver ETFs that are not leveraged will have price movements similar to that of spot silver at 5%. The chances of losing a lot of money on these ETFs are slim as long as the investor keeps a watchful eye and doesn't let his or her losses grow too large before selling. There are also leveraged silver ETFs which provide for greater volatility. Many are 3x times leveraged, which means if spot silver were to gain 5% these 3x leveraged ETFs would make a move closer to 15%, three times the price movement of spot silver. Leveraged ETFs are more volatile, which means they are also much riskier. There's more money to be made in less time with these ETFs, but it's also easier to lose money much faster when the trade goes against you.

One interesting thing about silver (and gold) ETFs is that many of them also have an inverse ETF to match it. The inverse ETF trades on the short side. For example, NUGT is a gold ETF that you can buy when you want to "go long" and buy shares based on the speculation that the price of gold will increase. NUGT's inverse ETF is DUST, which you would buy if you want to "sell short" and buy shares based on the speculation that the price of gold will drop. This is handy because it allows investors to both go long and sell short on a commodity without having a margin account and short selling capabilities. This is great for anyone who doesn't want to get involved with margin or short selling. When selling short, it's possible to not only lose your entire investment, but also to go into debt. In theory the share price of a stock can rise to infinity, so if an investor is shorting that stock and can't buy shares to "cover" in time when the share prices rises against them, a single bad trade can send them heavily into debt. Short selling is bad news for beginning traders and investors, but inverse ETFs allow the investor to bet against a commodity's price without truly selling short.

One major drawback with ETFs is that they tend to experience decay over time. Decay is when the share price continues to drop over time despite the fact that the commodity it represents may have risen significantly over that same time period. For example, let's say gold rises to $1,350 and NUGT rises to $30 in tandem, then gold dips to $1,295 and NUGT follows by dropping to $20. Gold moves slowly, so we'll say it takes two months for gold to reach $1,350 again. By the time it's back to that price, NUGT will have risen to $26, let's say. Then gold dips again, rises again, and then NUGT is back up to only $22 while gold reaches $1,350 for the third time in several months. This is decay. Over time ETFs tend to lose value, making them poor vehicles for long-term investment. If you're looking to day trade or swing trade silver or gold over a period of a few days, maybe even a week or more, ETFs are a great, but avoid using them as vehicles for long-term investment.

Here's a list of some of the top silver ETFs and their ticker symbols if you're interested in trading them.

- VelocityShares 3x Long Silver ETN (USLV)
- ProShares Ultra Silver (AGQ)
- iShares Silver Trust (SLV)
- Global X Silver Miners ETF (SIL)
- Credit Suisse X-Links Silver CovCall ETN (SLVO)
- iShares MSGI Global Silver Miners ETF (SLVP)
- VelocityShares 3x Inverse Silver ETN (DSLV)
- ProShares UltraShort Silver (ZSL)

Keep your losses minimal by getting out of a trade that goes against you, and remember that the longer you stay in a silver ETF, the more likely you're going to lose money due to decay. This may be true no matter how strong the price of silver may be. Remember that ETFs may be useful trading vehicles but they are not good choices for investment.

Futures Contracts and Options

Futures contracts and options are similar to ETFs in that they are paper derivatives that also use leverage. Options and futures contracts are more difficult to understand and to trade than stocks and ETFs so they're not the best choices for a beginning trader or investor.

Futures contracts are unique in that the buyer of a contract can call for the delivery of the underlying asset when the contract expires. Delivery doesn't always occur, as in a similar vein that in years past, holders of currency didn't always demand delivery of the gold that was represented by the currency. The paper trades around, moving from hand to hand. In the case of silver, if all the holders of the paper silver were to demand delivery, they'd soon discover that the silver doesn't exist! There's not enough of it to fulfill all the contracts just as there wasn't enough gold in the bank vaults to cover all the currency during the days of the Gold Standard. Paper derivatives are not real assets, and especially in the case of silver (and gold) derivatives, they're not wise long-term investments.

Investing In Silver

If you're interested in investing in silver and you're ready to get started, the great news is that it's one of the easiest and cheapest investments a person can make. The price of silver right this moment is $15.54 an ounce, so if you want to buy some silver all you need is $15.54. In fact, you don't even need that much. If you're okay with buying what the industry calls "junk silver" you can buy some for about $1.12 today. Prices change daily, but that's what you're looking at to buy a circulated 1964 Roosevelt silver dime today. That $1.12 silver dime was worth $3.53 in 2011, so the potential is there to make profits on even the tiniest of silver investments.

One of the most beautiful things about investing in silver is how ridiculously cheap it is right now. What else can you begin to invest in with only $1.12? With a commission-free trading cell phone application, you could find a cheap enough penny stock and buy a few shares, but the potential for growth isn't as strong as when buying silver, and you'll have nothing to show for it other than a number on a computer screen, the same as the "paper" we've been discussing for most of this book. Whether you start with $1 or $1,000, the potential behind silver is unlike anything else available today. No matter how much you buy, silver prices are unlikely to drop much lower than they are right now. At these price levels, silver is an inexpensive and low-risk investment, perfect for the beginning investor.

Physical is the Way!

If you're investing in silver for the long haul, as opposed to trading it short-term, physical silver is the way to go. Any "paper" you may be holding onto in place of physical silver is practically no different than the cash in your wallet. The "value" is merely in what the paper represents, the physical silver itself. So why not cut out the middle and focus only on the silver? If the silver derivatives market were to come tumbling down, everyone would be clamoring for physical silver and it would disappear quickly since there's not enough of it to back all the paper that trades on its behalf. The silver derivatives market is a house of cards, and if/when that house comes tumbling down, the sturdy foundation of physical silver will still hold strong beneath it.

If you're paying storage fees for a business or investment pool to store silver for you, the chances are good that you're paying for them to store absolutely nothing! Since the silver you're buying from one of these businesses is paper silver that doesn't exist, you're paying them to store silver that doesn't exist. It's a scam. The derivatives market makes it much easier for scammers to swindle the unsuspecting public. Buying and storing physical silver yourself is the safest approach. Physical silver beats out all other investment methods. You know exactly what you're buying, you know how much you're buying, you can hold it in your hand, so you know it exists and it's yours. It's relatively easy to count, keep track of, and transport. You can store a whole hoard of silver in a small floor safe or wall safe and no one will ever know it's there. You can buy a few pieces of junk silver and leave them out on your desk or coffee table and if a thief breaks into your home, he won't even know the $1.80 in loose change you left lying out is really worth over $20. Most people have no idea silver is worth anything at all. This decreases the odds of theft. Thieves rarely break into houses for a few dollars in loose change, or a silver eagle that has a face value of $1.00. Thieves tend to steal what they know is valuable and liquid, like the Playstation 4.

Another benefit of having physical silver is that it's nearly indestructible. Silver has a melting point of 1,763 degrees Fahrenheit. Your entire house could burn down, your cash will go up in flames, but your silver will still be there, mostly unscathed. The value is in the silver weight, not the appearance of the coins or bars, so the value will not have diminished whatsoever.

Silver is real money and if you're going to collect it, you'll want to keep it safe somewhere that is easily accessible to you. The safe deposit box at the bank is one option, but even then it has risks. If you have a safe or know a trusted someone who has a safe, that will probably be your best option for keeping physical silver. The easier you are able to access it, the smoother things will go when the times come for you to sell it.

There's nothing wrong with saving cash, building a stock portfolio, or trading gold and silver ETFs. These can all be great investments strategies. Investing in silver doesn't mean you should avoid all other investments. All it means is that silver's time is coming, and when it comes, you want to have physical silver, the safest and most liquid way to invest in the precious metal.

When to Buy?

The best time to buy silver is right now! Okay, the best time to buy silver was probably in the late 1990's and early 2000's, but if you did not, don't worry, because the *next* best time to buy silver is right now. Silver has been beaten down since 2011. Silver is lower right now than it was during most of 2008, 2009, 2010, 2011, 2012, 2013, 2014, 2015, 2016, and 2017. Even half of 2018 showed silver holding above $16. Meanwhile, the silver supply has decreased significantly over that time. Silver has been selling off since 2011 and is cheap and unloved right now.

One excellent piece of advice on when to buy is to buy the price dips. In July 2018 the price of silver was between $15.50 and $16 but it dipped down to about $14 in September 2018. Silver around $14 was the cheapest price we've seen since 2009, nearly a full decade. The dip to $14 was the best buy, but anywhere around these levels is cheap compared to where silver has been and where it may go from here.

Many investors keep buying silver all along the way, waiting for dips if they can, but knowing that silver has tremendous potential that has barely ever been tapped. Many investors see silver as money, and if the price per ounce drops after they buy some, they don't mind. They know the downside risk is limited, yet the potential to the upside is practically unlimited. Some investors continue to buy no matter where the price is headed. It drops, they buy. It goes up, they buy. Many simply want to own as much as possible, knowing the shortage could start showing itself any day.

The next best time to buy silver is whenever you can afford it. If you're barely scraping by, struggling to feed yourself, it may not be the best time to buy silver, unless you can keep your purchases minimal so that you can still afford to pay the bills. This is where silver shines brightly as an investment. Many people cannot go out and buy rental property. Many cannot go out and buy an ounce of gold at $1,322. Even a 1/10th of an ounce of gold will cost about $132, not counting premiums. If you're struggling to feed yourself, these investments are not realistic. However, even if times are tight and you're struggling to survive, chances are pretty good that you'll be able to part with a dollar or two every week to buy some junk silver coins.

The best time to buy silver is whenever you can!

Where to Buy?

There are many great ways to buy precious metals. We'll go over some of the most common places to buy them and the pros and cons of each. This is only a partial list, covering the places that generally have a good selection and good prices.

Coin Shops

It depends on the individual business, but coin shops are probably your best bet for purchasing silver bullion. The great thing about buying from coin shops is that you can have a one-on-one conversation with the dealer, get to know them, perhaps even befriend them. The dealer will get to know you, what you're interested in, and may begin to look out for items they know you might be looking for. Many other methods for purchasing silver bullion are impersonal and relatively uninteresting. If you're entering a coin shop once a month, however, you're bound to develop a bit of a relationship with the owner, which is a more comfortable feeling when you're coughing up your hard-earned cash.

Another great aspect of buying from coin shops is that you can look around, see what the shop has to offer, check out the pricing on certain items, and learn about precious metals, coins, and currency. The more you know about numismatics, the better informed you'll be when purchasing silver as an investment. Many precious metals investors began as coin collectors. Many valuable numismatic coins are silver coins, so an interest in numismatics can soon develop into an interest in precious metals, and vice versa.

Coin shops are more likely to have a large array of both junk silver coins and bullion rounds, ingots, and bars. You'll be able to ask the owner questions about anything and they'll be happy to answer you, appreciating your interest. Someone who is interested enough to ask questions is a good candidate for turning into a repeat customer, especially if the owner offers sincere and informative answers. Coin shops may sell out of certain items, and some time may pass before they have those items in stock again, but generally speaking, they will have a wide selection, offering something for everyone on any budget. From a single 1964 Roosevelt silver dime, to gold bars worth thousands of dollars, a coin shop is likely to have whatever you're looking for.

One drawback of coin shops is that you won't find one in every single town. You may have to make a bit of a trek to find one, but once you have found one, try stopping in a few times and making a few smaller purchases to get an idea of how you interact with the owner. If you become a repeat customer, the owner may even begin to cut you deals or save you a few bucks here and there. Especially if you plan to buy precious metals frequently. Having a friend in the business can save you time and money.

Watch out for coin shop owners that try to sell you numismatic coins when you tell them you're looking for junk silver or silver bullion. Numismatic coins are an entirely different ballgame (which we'll get to later) and they can come with extremely steep premiums, even when priced appropriately. Also watch out for a coin shop owner trying to up-sell you to a larger quantity of silver than what you ask for. If you tell them you're looking for one or two silver rounds and the dealer tries to sell you a 10 ounce silver bar, that dealer may not be listening to you because he or she wants to make more money. Honest dealers are also reputable dealers, and chances are they have plenty of business coming in, therefore they have no desire to swindle you for short-term cash because it may ruin their reputation and cripple long-term revenue.

Antique Shops

Finding silver at antique shops is hit or miss. They're more likely to have numismatic coins and junk silver than silver bullion rounds and bars. Many antique shops don't carry coins or precious metals at all, but the ones that do often carry older coins, as is more in line with antiques. Much of the silver bullion that is sold and traded isn't old, especially silver eagles, which have only been minted since 1986.

While it may be tough to find silver at antique shops, often the ones who do carry silver coinage have great prices. If coins aren't their specialty, they're not expecting to make much money from what they carry, so they often have affordable prices in order to move the stock. The most common silver coins you'll find at antique shops will be junk silver from 1964 and earlier, Morgan and Peace dollars, and Kennedy half dollars prior to 1970. You may occasionally find silver eagles at antique shops, but they're unlikely to carry much beyond that in terms of silver bullion.

On the other hand, antique shops can be a great place to find sterling silver, another method of collecting that we'll delve into more deeply later.

Online Bullion Dealers

There are plenty of precious metals dealers that conduct business online. By searching their websites, you can find excellent deals on silver rounds of varying sizes from all over the world, such as American silver eagles, Mexican Libertads, Austrian Philharmonics, and Chinese silver pandas. Many online dealers also have Morgan and Peace dollars, silver bars of varying weights, from one ounce to one kilogram. They have hand-poured bars, commemoratives, junk silver coins, and so much more.

Online bullion dealers typically do such high volume that they can afford to keep prices low. Their prices vary greatly, but most tend to offer reduced pricing when buying larger quantities. When purchasing American silver eagles, for example, the American Precious Metals Exchange (APMEX) might charge $20.22 per silver eagle when purchasing 1-19 silver eagles, but when buying 20-99 eagles, the price per eagle might drop to $19.91.

Prices also vary based on whether the buyer is paying by credit card, PayPal, or check. Some online dealers also accept Bitcoin as a form of payment. Prices vary and change frequently, as silver prices change daily. Below is a list of some of the biggest and most reputable online precious metals dealers. Check out their websites, compare prices, and search through what each dealer carries to get an idea of which you prefer.

- Kitco (www.kitco.com)
- American Precious Metals Exchange (www.apmex.com)
- Provident Metals (www.providentmetals.com)
- JM Bullion (www.jmbullion.com)
- Gold & Silver Inc. (www.goldsilver.com)

There are many more precious metals dealers online, and if you search around you may find one you like better. This list is only a small selection of some of the biggest dealers to help you get started. When purchasing precious metals online, it's safest and generally cheaper to go with a well-known, reputable dealer.

eBay

This behemoth of an online auction house has some good deals on silver and is a great alternative for anyone who is unable to purchase precious metals from local coin shops or online bullion dealers. However, not all the deals offered on eBay are good. It takes careful scrutiny to weed out the good deals from the bad. That's not to say that any dealers on eBay are trying to swindle anyone, it's a matter of the fundamentals being different.

To begin with, spot silver prices can change every minute, every second, whereas eBay auctions and "Buy It Now" sales tend to run for a period of a few days or more. This means that the spot price of silver can drop significantly in an hour, in a day or more, while the listed price on the eBay auction remains the same without being adjusted to reflect the lower spot price of silver. This can lead to a buyer paying significantly more than they'd pay elsewhere, especially when buying in quantity. If the price of a silver eagle is set to $21 on eBay (including shipping) while the silver price hovers around $15.75, it may not be such a bad deal. However, if silver then falls to $14.00 that same day and someone buys 100 silver eagles at $21 each, it's no longer such an attractive deal. Of course, this can also be used to a buyer's benefit should the spot price of silver rise significantly before the eBay listing can follow. The multitude of variables and price fluctuations can make it much more difficult to sift through and find the good deals.

Another drawback of buying silver bullion off eBay is that the buyer isn't likely to get reduced pricing when buying in quantity. Often the "Buy It Now" sales have a fixed price for a quantity of one and buying more than one won't reduce that price per unit. Especially if the sale offers free shipping, which sounds great and *can* be a benefit in some cases, but then the seller will not be able to combine shipping when the buyer purchases larger quantities. There are many auctions and "Buy It Now" sales that are excellent buying opportunities, but for the beginning investor, it will be more difficult to find these great deals among the not-so-great deals. By the same token, for anyone with enough time on their hands and the desire to learn, studying precious metals and their listed prices on eBay is an excellent way to learn the market, to see what's in demand, and to learn how to identify the good deals from the bad.

One of the great things about eBay when it comes to precious metals is that it's accessible to those who may not have a local coin shop and may feel uncomfortable ordering from a bulk precious metals dealer online. Buyers might pay a bit more purchasing from eBay, but absolutely anything they might be looking for is there for the buying. For anyone on a budget, eBay is a great option. There's no minimum purchase, so anyone short on cash who wants to start investing in silver can buy a single Roosevelt silver dime from 1964 for about $2.15 today, including free shipping. That dime may be worth only $1.11 today, but it's an affordable option for most people. If they have $10 to spend, they may be able to buy five Roosevelt silver dimes for $10, paying only $2 per dime. It depends on the deals that are available from day to day.

Silver and gold bullion typically sell for top dollar on eBay, a strong indicator of the current demand. Even auctions or "But It Now" sales that seem overpriced still sell. This indicates strong demand. Silver and gold bullion, as well as numismatic coins all seem to sell for great prices. The premiums that dealers place on precious metals to turn a profit seems to have carried over to eBay. If a silver eagle is worth

$15.40 in silver weight, the premium is included on eBay, bringing the price closer to $20 - $21 with premium and "free" shipping. If anything, premiums seem to be a bit higher on eBay than local coin shop or bulk online precious metals dealers. eBay may be a great option for purchasing silver, but it's not likely to be the cheapest option. On the other hand, eBay is one of the best options when looking to *sell* coins and precious metals, as we'll discuss shortly. Since eBay tends to fetch top dollar for silver and gold, that may make it the best option for people looking to sell, even when taking into account the fees for eBay and PayPal.

The most important thing to remember with eBay, whether buying or selling, is that the more you shop around and the more time you spend searching through the different listings, the more likely you are to find great deals when you buy, and to fetch top dollar when you sell.

Friends

If you have friends looking to sell their silver or gold, convince them not to! If they insist, however, purchasing precious metals from a friend is an excellent option. Often your friends will not know the value of what they're looking to sell, and they may be nervous taking it to a dealer or coin shop. Even if the dealer offers a good price, chances are it's only going to be a percentage of the spot price of the metal. Dealers have to earn a living, so they buy for a small percentage under the metal's current spot value, and sell for a premium above spot value to the next buyer. Buying silver directly from friends eliminates the middleman and the pricing scale. If you're buying from a friend, at least offer them the correct price for the current spot value of silver. This way, they get more money than the dealer would have paid, and you'll pick up the silver for less money than the dealer would have charged. In this scenario, only the dealer misses out, but most bullion dealers deal in volume and have no shortage of other buyers and sellers to profit from.

The drawback of buying precious metals from friends is that they're unlikely to have everything you're looking for, and what they do have will be in finite amounts. Friends won't have unlimited quantities of coins, rounds, and bars to sell, so buying from them will be sporadic, but when they *are* looking to sell, it can be a WIN-WIN situation for both parties.

What to Buy?

There are a few important questions to ask when deciding what to buy. The first question is what interests you? If you're patriotic, you may want to collect bullion from your own country. If you're Canadian, you may want to stick to Canadian maple leaf rounds. If you're taken by a particular foreign country, you may want to collect bullion from that country. How about collecting a little from every country that offers its own silver bullion? Thanks to the internet, this will be easy, as everything is right there at your fingertips. If you only want the silver and you're not concerned with which nation your bullion comes from, try going with whatever is cheapest and looks interesting.

What form of silver bullion are you looking for? If you're a coin collector, silver rounds, junk silver coinage, and old silver Morgan and Peace dollars might be your thing. The beauty of collecting old, worn Morgan and Peace dollars is that not only do you get the silver weight (0.77344 ounce), you also get a numismatic coin that has circulated for decades and has countless stories to tell. Many of these coins are also antiques, which will appeal to collectors of all things old and interesting. Badly worn Morgan and Peace dollars are often considered culls, meaning their collector value is gone, which means the buyer will pay a minimal numismatic premium, if any.

The next question to ask is what are your goals? Many people who get into silver bullion simply want to have a little bit lying around for a rainy day. Maybe someone in their family was a collector and piqued their interest. They're not trying to collect 1,000 ounces of silver, they only want a few silver dollars and some interesting old silver coins, like Barber dimes or Walking Liberty half dollars. Some people have no interest in becoming a serious collector, all they want is a few interesting coins to keep on hand. Others may have a diverse investment portfolio and they want to have some silver and gold to diversify even further. Then some people are serious "silver stackers" and want to collect as much as they can get their hands on. Maybe they've learned about the unique properties and opportunities with silver and they want to pack as much away as possible, anticipating large profits in the future with the rise of precious metals prices. Some people have little faith in fiat currency and expect that silver and gold will reclaim their place as sound money one day, and they want to be prepared for when that day comes. How much silver do you want to own, and for what purpose? Decide what your goals are and you'll be able to determine what you need to do to reach them.

The last question to ask is what's your budget? How much are you willing to spend on silver? Are you able to put a small portion of your income aside each week or each month? How much are you willing to set aside? It could be a specified dollar amount or a percentage of your weekly paycheck. Do you already have a certain amount you're setting aside each week for general investments? Do you want to use a portion of that to buy silver, or are you interested in focusing all of your investment funds on precious metals? Even if you set $5 aside every week to buy silver, you'll have about 17 ounces by the end of the year at today's silver prices. If you can part with $20 each week for silver purchases, you'll have around 70 ounces by the end of a year at today's prices. If you're not able to set a specific dollar amount aside each week, maybe buying a small amount of silver each will be easier. If you buy only two silver dimes a week, that'll only run you about $2.18. Most people can afford to part with $2.18 each week. At the end of the year, you'll have 104 dimes and about 7.5 ounces of silver. It's not much, but it's better than nothing. If silver hits $50 by the end of the year, you'll have a hefty profit, and you won't have to look back on the year *wishing* you'd bought some silver.

How Much to Buy?

How much silver to buy will largely depend on your goals and your budget. Let's say you're looking to own a total of 100 ounces by the end of the year. How much money will you need to shell out each week to reach that goal? Many investors who are in it for the long haul don't worry much about the day-to-day price fluctuations. They don't worry about how much they'll buy this year or how much they own already. Many investors simply want to own as much silver as possible, so they "just keep stacking." They may buy a single silver round one week and a ten ounce bar the next. There's no pattern behind their purchases, they keep stacking no matter what. They don't care that they bought silver above $30 an ounce and it's now barely above $15. They're happy to purchase silver at practically any price because they're in it for the long run and they know their purchase prices will average out over time. For many investors who believe silver and gold to be sound money, *real* money, they're happy to own as much as they can, and they believe the act of turning fiat currency into sound money is worth it at any price.

A good rule is to buy as much silver as you can without letting it affect your life. Once all expenses are taken care of, if you only have $100 left per month in disposable income, it's not a wise decision to spend all of that on silver. On the other hand, if you have $1,000 each month in disposable income after all your expenses are paid, buying only one ounce of silver a month won't cut it if you're looking for big profits with the coming rise in precious metals prices. Decide what your goals are, decide what your budget is, then buy however much silver you can while still fitting within these parameters. You can change your goals and your budget at any time, and you may wish to make adjustments as you discover what works for you

Where to Keep It?

Deciding where to keep your silver depends on many factors. Having a safe place in your home to hoard your stacks will ensure you have easy access whenever you want to count it or add to it. The ideal storage space will be somewhere that is concealed and safe from theft. If you live alone, or with people you trust completely, a good hiding place may be all you need. If you're worried about break-ins and theft, a safe may be your best option. Floor safes and wall safes are excellent because they can be concealed, and even if discovered, they're exceptionally difficult to break into or remove from the home. Regular safes are great as well, as not only are they hard to break into, but they're also heavy and difficult to pick up and carry away. The heavier the safe, the less likely a thief will be able to leave with it. In order to access the contents, they'll have to break into it on the premises and the odds of the average burglar having the skill and time to break into a safe on the premises are slim.

Lockboxes are not the best option for storing valuables such as silver bullion. Not only are lockboxes incredibly light weight and easy to carry away, they're also fairly easy to break into. Anyone with a hammer or a large rock can break into a lockbox, and that's assuming it's even locked to begin with. Additionally, most people will be able to recognize a lockbox, which is a dead giveaway that there's likely to be something valuable inside. They're prime candidates for a thief to simply tuck under his arm and flee the scene with to break open later. If you can't afford a good safe, don't even bother buying a lockbox—unless you're going to hide it well or fill it with worthless items to act as a diversion in case of theft.

If you're worried about theft, you may want to consider asking a trusted friend or relative who has a safe if they'd be willing to let you store your precious metals there. Silver doesn't require much storage space, with ten 10 ounce bars (100 ounces) hardly taking up more space than a typical paperback novel. The problem with storing your precious metals at the home of a trusted friend or relative is that you won't have as easy access to your hoard as you would were it stored in your own home. It will take extra time and energy whenever you want to count your stacks or add to them. The further your friend or relative lives from you, the less convenient it will be to make regular visits. There's also the possibility that as your stacks grow, the person storing your collection may eventually decide they need that space for their own st.orage needs. You'll want to take all of this into account when deciding whether to store your collection with someone else for safekeeping.

Another option is storing your silver in a safe deposit box. Your silver will certainly be safe from theft, but you'll have limited access to it. It's not practical for most silver stackers to keep their silver in a safe deposit box. If they make frequent silver purchases, they're going to have to make frequent bank visits. Whenever they want to tally up their silver, they'll need to take the time inside the safe at the bank to do the tallying. Banks also have limited hours, so anyone wanting to access their silver inside a safe deposit box may have to wait hours or even days to gain access. Safe deposit boxes are also rather small and are not ideal for storing precious metals. Storing a few gold coins in a safe deposit box may prove to be a good idea, but if you're looking to deposit 1,000 ounces of silver bullion, it will not be practical. What happens when the box is full? Open another safe deposit box? Banks charge fees for safe deposit boxes, so for an investor looking to place a few gold coins, it may be worthwhile, but for a serious silver stacker looking to add to their collection on a regular basis, safe deposit boxes aren't practical.

If you have the room and the budget for a personal safe, that will prove to be your safest and most convenient option. Look for a safe that will leave your collection plenty of room to grow. There's no sense in buying a small safe, filling it with silver, then having to buy yet another, larger safe as your silver stacks grow. Buy the largest, heaviest safe you can afford and store, then secure it to the floor with bolts if you can.

When to Sell?

The most difficult question of all to answer is when to sell your silver. Only you can make that decision. Some investors sell when they have a decent profit. Others sell when they've doubled or tripled their money, which can take years or decades. Some investors are waiting for that specific dollar amount, such as $50 silver, $100 silver, or $1,000 silver. Then you have investors who have little faith in fiat currency and see silver and gold as the only true money. They may *never* sell, believing that one day the value of silver and gold will no longer be measured in terms of a dollar amount. Perhaps they're waiting for hyperinflation or total economic meltdown, so that instead of pushing a wheelbarrow full of worthless paper currency down the street to buy a loaf of bread, they'll carry a single Roosevelt silver dime in their pocket to the store to buy a loaf of bread. Or maybe they're waiting until they can trade their precious metals in for the next big investment that's currently on the upswing.

When deciding the right time to sell, revisit your goals. What are you in this for? What is your plan, your endgame? How close are you to realizing your goals? When silver reached $20 per ounce in early 2008, the proprietor at the nearest coin shop watched as silver investors brought in Whitman coin books filled with Morgan dollars, Peace dollars, and half dollars. Many of those investors were old-timers who'd been collecting for decades. It's safe to assume that many of those investors had been buying silver since the 1970's made returns upward of 1000%. If they'd bought most of that silver in the 1990's, many of them still had 400% or 500% returns. They sold at $20 and made big profits and walked away thinking they had cleaned up. Little did they know that only three years later, in early 2011, silver would hit $49.

On the other hand, investors who bought silver over $40 looking to sell above $100 never got that chance. They may have held onto those "losses" if they're in it for the long haul, but if not, they probably took heavy losses around the $30's or even the $20's. Those burned investors may have even vowed never to bother with silver and gold again.

When to sell is the most difficult question to answer because no one knows! If you're in it for short-term profits, sell when you have a decent profit. If you're in it for the long run, then wait until you feel the time is right and your goals have been reached. It may be a matter of months or even years. No one knows when silver will make its move, but as we've discussed, everything is lined up, waiting for the initial push to launch silver prices upward, in search of fair market value.

Where to Sell?

When you're ready to sell some or all of your silver, you'll want to get top dollar for it. The best places to sell your precious metals aren't necessarily going to be the same as the best places to buy. Let's take a look at some of the different places that may be good candidates for consideration when deciding where to sell.

Coin Shops

While coin shops may be one of the best places to buy silver, they're not your best option when it comes to selling. Coin shops need to make a profit, and in doing so, they must sell their silver above spot prices and buy their silver below spot prices. The average reputable coin shop will pay somewhere between 85% and 90% of the melt value of silver on any given day. If a seller walks in with an American silver eagle, and the spot price of silver is $15.00 that day, the coin shop will pay that seller around $12.75 to $13.50 for that silver eagle. If that same seller walks out the door in regret, turns back around to immediately buy back that same silver eagle, the coin shop will charge around $18 to $20. Coin shops buy for a percentage and sell for a premium. This is how they make money, it's standard practice in the industry.

Selling precious metals back to a coin dealer will seldom be a wise move. However, if you need money fast and you bought the silver years ago for $10 per ounce, selling to coin shops can be convenient in a pinch. Otherwise, you'll get more money for your silver by selling it elsewhere. If you must sell to a coin shop or bullion dealer, shop around. Call ahead and ask what percentage of melt they pay. Dealers that pay more than 90% are rare but they do exist. If you must sell to a dealer or coin shop and you find one that pays 91% of melt value (or higher), that will probably be the best rate you'll find.

eBay

Your current best option for getting top dollar when selling your silver is eBay. Demand is high on eBay and many silver numismatic coins as well as silver bullion sell for prices at or above their current retail market values. eBay is the best and most convenient option for many silver investors who know that the opportunity for excellent deals is there, ready and waiting. Coins are fairly cheap to ship, especially if it's only a single coin being sent. Coins stand alone when it comes to small items that can have great value, that can also be shipped for minimal costs.

For anyone looking to sell silver and gold on eBay, it's not difficult to make the sale for a price that includes a premium, pay eBay and PayPal fees, pay for shipping, and still walk away with more currency in your pocket than the coin shop would have given. The combination of convenience, accessibility, and high prices paid will be tough to beat elsewhere. Also, no matter what sort of volume you're looking to move, there will be no shortage of buyers here. However much you're looking to sell, you'll have no problems unloading it on eBay.

Friends and Other Investors

One of the most promising ways to sell silver is to friends and other investors. Knowledgeable investors will be well aware of the fact that when buying from coin shops, they have to pay premiums, when buying off eBay, they'll have to pay premiums *and* shipping fees—even if the seller claims "free shipping", they're in business to make money and those shipping fees will be in the sale price somewhere. When selling to other investors, you should be able to fetch a dollar amount that will please both you and the buyer. In this way, you won't have to wait for auction listings, PayPal deposits, or anything else. If both parties have basic knowledge of silver bullion, both should be able to walk away happy, knowing they saved time, money, and hassle.

How Much to Sell?

Only you can decide how much of your silver you will sell. Once again, it depends on your goals. If you're looking for short-term profits, trading silver, rather than investing might be better for you. Trading silver is riskier, but takes no long-term commitment. If you're in it for the long run, however, you may want to sell a percentage of your silver to lock in some profits and then hold onto the rest. Some investors sell a percentage of their silver when they've reached an attractive profit, then they save the rest, perhaps selling more at the next pricing milestone. For example, they may be planning to sell 10% of their silver when the price reaches $50, then another 10% when the price reaches $100 and so on. By selling in increments, they have more control over their profits, making sure to lock in gains incrementally along the way. If they've purchased their silver in a similar manner, buying smaller amounts on a regular basis over time, then selling periodically at certain price levels, they'll minimize their chances of realizing any large losses. They may also reduce their chances of making exceptionally large profit percentages (if they had bought all their silver at $5 and sold all of it at $49), but they'll minimize risk and maximize profit potential long-term.

For investors who are devout silver stackers, bent on holding on long-term for maximum possible gains, they may not want to sell any silver at all. Many investors who are long-term silver stackers are waiting for an unprecedented silver price, such as $1,000 before they'll sell a single ounce. Those investors often buy weekly or monthly no matter what the price of silver is. All they want is to own as much silver as possible so that when the time comes, they can make as much money as possible. When the price rises to higher levels, such as $25 to $35 per ounce or more, they buy. When the price drops to lows of $14 to $16, they buy as much as they can. Other long-term investors buy the same amount of silver every week or every month, no matter what the price of silver is at that time.

No one can tell you how much of your silver to sell. By devising a plan for your own investments and sticking to that plan, adjusting when necessary, you'll know when the time is right for you. You may want to sell all your precious metals and invest in an opportunity with even better profit potential. It's not wise to be married to any one form of investment as any investment could fall through at any time. It's understandable to go with the investment that has the greatest future profit potential, but at this time, what better opportunities than silver and gold are out there?

Understanding Premiums

The mint takes gold and silver, melts them down, and makes beautiful rounds and bars of varying weight for investors to buy. These rounds and bars come in specific weights, with the total amount of fine silver or gold included on each piece. The mint then distributes these pieces to dealers around the world. In order for the mint to make a profit, they must sell each piece for more than their purchase price for the metals. Minting rounds and bars takes time and work, and at the end of the day, the mint must turn a profit by selling the metal to dealers at a mark-up. This is known as a premium. The premium a bullion dealer pays when purchasing from the mint is about $1 to $2 above the spot price for the metal. Which means if the spot price of silver is $15, the bullion dealer must pay the mint $16 or $17 per silver round. If the dealer owns silver rounds for $16 or $17 each, that dealer must then sell at a higher premium in order to turn a profit. This is why when the average precious metals buyer walks into a coin shop and asks for one American silver eagle, that buyer will pay somewhere between $18 and $20 for that silver even though the spot price for the metal is $15.

For a buyer walking into a coin shop looking to buy silver, that buyer should expect to pay a certain premium for each item they purchase. Premiums are priced differently, often determined by how much work went into producing each individual piece of silver. Let's say the spot price of silver is $15 on the day the buyer wants to purchase a few different pieces of silver. That buyer can expect to pay $3 to $5 premium for a one ounce American silver eagle from the United States Mint. This means an average of $4 premium per ounce when purchasing silver eagles. When purchasing in quantity, that buyer *may* get a deal if the dealer is feeling generous, but for the most part, if the buyer wants 10 silver eagles, he will have to pay that $4 premium per eagle. The buyer also asks for a generic silver round, not from the United States Mint. That generic silver round will likely carry a premium of somewhere between $2 and $4, making the average premium $3 per ounce when purchasing a generic silver round. Let's say the buyer also asks for a 10 ounce silver bar. The premium on that bar might be about $20 or $25, meaning $2 to $2.50 per ounce of silver. A 20 ounce bar might carry a premium of $30 to $40, meaning $1.50 to $2 per ounce. Generally speaking, the heavier the piece of silver being purchased, the less the premiums will be per ounce. This is due, in part, to the fact that producing a 20 ounce bar requires essentially the same amount of labor to produce a one ounce round or bar. If you're looking to save money when purchasing silver and gold bullion, you'll want to go with larger pieces of silver, such as 10 and 20 ounce bars.

Junk silver tends to carry the lowest premiums, if any. Junk silver is worn, busted-up coins that have been heavily circulated and no longer carry any numismatic value. The value that remains is solely the intrinsic value: the silver contained within the coin. Junk silver has a specified unit of the precious metal within, and it is also still legal tender. The mint produced these coins many decades ago. The mint doesn't need to turn a profit from junk silver by selling to a dealer. The dealer doesn't necessarily have to sell junk silver for a premium because chances are that dealer purchased the junk silver for the standard 85-90%. The dealer's profit was made when they purchased the junk silver, and therefore they may not feel the need to sell for a premium. Even if a particular dealer *does* sell junk silver for a small premium, the amount will be much less per ounce of silver than when purchasing bullion rounds and bars.

Understanding Bullion

Silver bullion comes in various weights and forms. Silver comes in rounds of one ounce, two ounces, three ounces, four ounces, five ounces, and ten ounces. Silver bars also come in all different sizes from one gram to one kilo and everything in between. Generally speaking, the smaller the piece of silver, the higher the premium per ounce it will carry. Silver is a relatively cheap metal (for now) so it will be cost prohibitive for most investors to buy silver in pieces of less than one ounce.

Silver bars tend to have lower premiums per ounce of silver than silver rounds, especially when the bar contains more than one ounce of silver. Hand-poured bars may have higher premiums than other bars because of the labor that goes into producing them. They're also more rare and arguably have a better look than the manufactured bars. Hand-poured bars are more unique and are a collector's item, which is another reason they may carry a higher premium. For collectors interested in precious metals for more than simple profits, having hand-poured bars in their collection can be fun and exciting.

Gold bullion is similar to silver, in that rounds and bars come in all different sizes and weights. Since gold is much more expensive than silver, gold bullion is sold in fractional amounts. The price of gold today reached $1,299 per ounce. Many people cannot afford an entire ounce of gold, so American gold eagles are also sold in fractional rounds of 1/10, 1/4, and 1/2 ounce. Since even the 1/10 ounce of gold will cost $129 today (not including premiums) gold is also sold in yet even smaller increments, such as one gram. A gram of gold today is worth about $42 (not including premiums) and is much more affordable for the average person than larger rounds or bars.

Understanding Numismatics

Numismatic coins that contain silver and gold are totally different than silver and gold bullion. It's important to understand the differences between the two so you don't spend excessive amounts of money on something you don't even want. "Numismatics" is the study of currency, or more specifically: the study of coins and paper money.

Numismatic coins are typically older coins that were minted to be used as circulating currency, and may or may not have actually circulated. Some of these older coins were kept in pristine condition over the years and may carry significant numismatic premiums based on condition, age, and rarity. Numismatic coins are valued for more than their silver or gold weights and many are sought after by collectors willing to pay significant numismatic premiums that are much higher than the silver or gold melt value.

Let's look at a few examples. Today a single American silver eagle will cost about $18 to $20 (including premiums) no matter the condition, and it contains a full ounce of fine silver. On the other hand, an 1881 Morgan silver dollar contains only 0.77344 ounces of silver, and in worn, circulated condition might carry a retail value of around $20 to $30, depending on the condition. A different Morgan dollar from the same year graded as MS-65 (mint state, 65 on a scale of 1-70) would be in pristine, uncirculated, mint state condition and could have a retail value in excess of $800. The coin only contains 0.77344 ounces of silver, or about $11.70 worth at today's spot silver prices, but the numismatic premium on that coin is so much higher because of the rarity and condition of the coin. If you're specifically looking for silver bullion, DO NOT let anyone talk you into buying such a numismatic coin.

The same $800 you might pay for that one Morgan silver dollar from 1881 is enough to purchase about 40 silver eagles. This is the difference between buying silver bullion and silver numismatic coins.

Another example would be an 1881-CC Morgan silver dollar. The CC means Carson City, Nevada where the coin was minted. The Carson City mint only operated from 1870-1885, and then again from 1889-1893, after which it closed permanently. During the time the Carson City mint was in operation, many of the coins minted there were produced in significantly smaller quantities than in other U.S. mints. There were 12,760,000 Morgan silver dollars minted at the San Francisco mint in 1881 (known as 1881-S), whereas there were only a mere 296,000 Morgan silver dollars minted in Carson City that same year. Since the 1881-CC Morgan dollars are so much rarer, their retail values reflect that rarity. A severely worn, low grade 1881-CC Morgan dollar might sell for $300 or more, but the same coin graded MS-65 would easily fetch over $1,000. The variables are unlimited for numismatic coins. An 1889-CC Morgan silver dollar, for example, is extremely rare and in MS-65 condition might sell for upwards of $500,000. An 1889-CC Morgan dollar in MS-68 condition sold at auction in 2009 for $531,876.[13] That coin contains about $11.70 worth of silver today.

A coin collector looking for a Morgan dollar from a specific year or grade would be happy to find what they're looking for in a coin shop. They may be happy to pay $50, $100, or $1,000 for a specific coin. That coin collector may also be happy to acquire more silver, but the main reason they would buy such a coin is for the numismatic value—the the age, the rarity, and the condition of the coin. That coin collector may also have a bullion collection, but rest assured that Morgan dollar will not be added to it. Also, a bullion collector with little interest in numismatic coins would not be interested in paying $100 for a Morgan dollar because they know they can get much more silver for their money when buying silver bullion instead of silver numismatic coins.

The potential problem here would be for someone new to coin collecting and precious metals investment. While most coin and bullion dealers are trustworthy in general terms (their business depends on their reputation) it is certainly possible they may try to up-sell someone who is unsure of what they're looking for. Someone who is new to coin collecting and precious metals investment might walk into a coin shop looking to leave with "some silver" may not know much about bullion or numismatics. If they tell the coin shop owner they are looking for "some silver" as an "investment" that coin shop owner has little information from the buyer to work with and might point the buyer to a beautiful, uncirculated Morgan silver dollar for $50. Not realizing that what the buyer is really looking for is silver bullion, the shop owner might explain why the Morgan is a wonderful choice. The buyer might purchase the Morgan dollar and leave happy. The shop owner is also happy—not only did they sell a coin for a good profit, they also watched another happy customer walk out the door with exactly what they were looking for. Had the buyer known to use the world "bullion" he may have walked out with more silver for less money. That's the problem for people who are new to precious metals investment. They may know nothing about bullion or numismatics and therefore they are leaving themselves open to spending more money and getting less silver. For anyone getting into precious metals or numismatic coin collecting, be sure to do as much research as possible so that you'll know *what* you're buying and *why* you're buying it before you slap your hard-earned money down onto the counter.

Numismatic coin collecting is a wonderful hobby, and can be incredibly rewarding and lucrative in its own right, but precious metals bullion collecting/investment is an entirely different game altogether. It's certainly possible to engage in both and to be successful in both separately, but you must know and understand the differences to avoid losing time and money and walking away with something you don't truly want. The more research you do and the more you learn about coin collecting and precious metals investment, the more adept you'll become at finding great deals on exactly the items you're looking for.

Junk Silver

Old silver coinage that is worn badly enough to no longer carry any numismatic premium or collector value beyond its intrinsic silver weight is known as "junk silver" or "90% silver." United States coins are the most common junk silver coins in the U.S. because they were all once circulating coins that were pulled out of circulation when the value of silver began to exceed the face value of the coins. The following is a list of U.S. coins that fall into the category of junk silver when they are new enough, worn enough, or plentiful enough to carry no value beyond the silver weight:

- U.S. quarters and dimes from the year 1964 and earlier
- U.S. half dollars from the year 1964 and earlier (90% silver)
- U.S. half dollars from 1965-1970 (40% silver)
- U.S. silver war nickels from 1942-1945 (35% silver)
- U.S. Morgan dollars and Peace dollars
- Silver coinage from other countries, such as Canada

Any of the above may or may not be considered junk silver, depending on the condition of the coin. Morgan and Peace dollars are often considered junk silver but may also carry a small numismatic premium. Smaller denomination coins such as dimes and quarters may also carry small premiums, but are likely to be the smallest premiums to be found on any silver coinage or bullion.

There are two things that should be noted with junk silver and the first is that junk silver coinage is 90% silver and 10% copper. This means that the silver in junk silver is not considered "investment grade." Investment grade silver is silver that is at least 99.9% pure. It's often called .999 silver. Presently this is not an issue as there is still plenty of investment grade silver to be purchased and used for industrial applications, however should there ever be a major shortage in industrial grade silver (as there may be in the near future), any junk silver to be used by industry would need to be refined — that is melted down to have the copper removed.

Many investors new to coin collecting and precious metals investment may be misled by terms like "melt value" and not realize these coins will not be melted down when they are traded in or sold. If *Investor A* walks into a coin shop and sells all of his or her junk silver to the shop, the coin shop will not turn around and sell those coins to a refinery to be melted. The coin shop will keep those coins on hand until *Investor B* enters the shop looking to buy junk silver. Then *Investor C* walks in to buy junk silver as well. It's in this way that junk silver changes hands — it trades around from investor to investor, from investor to coin or bullion dealer, and then from dealer back to investor. If you're looking to sell some junk silver but you're worried those coins will be melted down —

don't worry! The chances of your junk silver being melted
down after you sell it to a dealer are incredibly slim.

Troy Ounces

Bullion is always weighed in troy ounces. A troy ounce has
31.1 grams, as opposed to a regular ounce which has 28.35
grams. It's important for the precious metals investor to know
this so they can get an accurate count on the weight of
precious metals in their collection. The spot price of silver and
the amount of silver in numismatic coinage is also measured
in troy ounces. The silver content for bullion and coinage is as
follows:

- U.S. Silver Eagle (and other 1 ounce rounds)- 1 troy
  ounce
- U.S. Silver Dollar- 0.77344 troy ounce
- U.S. Silver Half Dollar- 0.36169 troy ounce
- U.S. Silver Quarter- 0.18 troy ounce
- U.S. Silver Dime- 0.072 troy ounce
- U.S. Silver War Nickel- 0.056 troy ounce

Many other coins also contain silver, such as U.S. half
dimes, U.S. three cent pieces, and various silver coinage from
other countries. However they are not bought or sold for their
silver weight, either because their numismatic value is higher
or because they contain such small amounts of silver, it makes

them impractical for exchanging hands as junk silver coinage. This is especially true for U.S. silver three cent pieces as they are so small and so uncommon, their numismatic value will almost always dwarf their silver value.

How to Follow Silver Prices

There are numerous websites that offer real-time quotes and charts for precious metals, but the number one most widely used site is GoldPrice.org. Established in 2002, GoldPrice.org offers live quotes for both silver and gold, and charts that date back to the 1970's. GoldPrice.org also offers candle charts, which reveal more detailed information about precious metals prices, and ratio charts. Using the ratio charts, you can track the ratios of Gold/Silver, DOW/Gold, and DOW/Silver. Using ratio charts, investors can get a better understanding of which investments are undervalued or overvalued. GoldPrice.org also offers spot silver and gold prices in a wide selection of different currencies, which is helpful for investors who are not from the United States.

Most precious metals dealers use GoldPrice.org for silver and gold prices, but for anyone looking for different options when checking spot prices, or in the unlikely chance that GoldPrice.org is inaccessible for any reason, Kitco.com and MoneyMetals.com also offer accurate spot prices for silver and gold.

.925 Sterling

Sterling silver, also known as ".925" or ".925 silver" for its purity of 92.5%, is most commonly used in jewelry and high-end silverware and tableware, such as tea sets, pots, goblets, pie servers, and various cutlery. Sterling silver is usually stamped ".925" and may also be stamped with a hallmark indicating where, when, or by whom the item was produced.

Collecting silver in the form of .925 sterling isn't necessarily better or worse than collecting silver in any other form. There are a few things to be mindful of, however, the first being that most items made of sterling silver are significantly heavier than a single ounce. In fact, most items made of sterling silver are relatively heavy by comparison to silver coinage or silver bullion, meaning that a single item crafted from sterling silver can weigh many ounces, even pounds, and therefore can easily be valued in the hundreds, if not thousands of dollars. Additionally, these items do not have a set weight, so anyone looking to buy or sell sterling silver would need to weigh each item and crunch some numbers to determine whether they're getting a good deal. Many of these items are also antiques and may carry extra value or premium, based on their age or where they were crafted. For example, it's possible for an antique sterling silver tea set to have a retail of $2,500 while the silver weight of the set is only valued at a few hundred dollars. These variables and wide price swings in the sterling silver market make it difficult for investors to gauge value, and to know what they're purchasing.

While coins and bars are bought and sold in specific weights which are minted or stamped onto the item, sterling silver has no specific weight and each item will need to be weighed and valued individually. When purchasing a coin or a bar, the buyer knows the exact weight and can easily determine the value. The weights are also in much smaller increments, so instead of investing hundreds or even thousands of dollars, an investor can hand over as little as $5 or $10 and leave with silver to add to their collection. For these reasons, purchasing sterling silver may prove to be impractical for anyone looking to collect silver as an investment.

Sterling silver jewelry is the exception, with many pieces such as earrings, bracelets, or necklaces being affordable for most. However, silver jewelry is rarely sold for its silver weight alone. Especially when buying brand new or high-end silver jewelry, the mark-up or premium may be excessive. For example, a pair of silver earrings may contain a mere 1/10 ounce of silver for the pair, or about $1.52 of the metal, but the earrings selling brand new might go for $20 to $30 or more. At such a steep mark-up, silver jewelry is not a good option for silver investors.

The most practical and cost-effective way for investors to purchase silver is junk silver coinage, or bullion in the form of rounds or bars. If you do wish to buy sterling silver, though, try doing it for the joy of collecting beautiful antique items with a rich history instead of the speculation of future profits.

Investing In Silver Without Getting Ripped Off

This is not to suggest that anyone will intentionally try to take advantage of would-be silver investors. There may be a few dealers out there looking to rip off unsuspecting newbie silver investors, but the majority of precious metals dealers want to remain in business and doing so means maintaining a good reputation.

One way an investor could get ripped off is having a lack of basic knowledge. We already discussed silver numismatic coins versus silver bullion, but it's worth mentioning again. A simple lack of knowledge can mean the difference between paying $20 for an ounce of silver and handing over $200 for less than an ounce of silver. It's one thing to be a coin collector looking for a specific coin, it's another to be a newbie silver investor looking for bullion. The coin dealer isn't taking advantage of anyone in such a scenario, but the buyer may be ripping himself off due to not knowing what he's looking for. A lack of knowledge can prove costly for any type of investor.

Should You Invest In Gold?

The focus of this book is silver because silver has the greatest potential for return on investment based on undervaluation, price suppression, and unique economic factors. However, that's not to say that gold doesn't have significant potential for profits. Gold is undervalued to some degree, and is also affected by many of the economic factors that pertain to silver. In *$10,000 Gold: Why Gold's Inevitable Rise Is the Investor's Safe Haven*, Nick Barisheff presents an excellent and well-researched case on why gold can reach *at least* $10,000 per ounce. With gold at around $1,292 today, that makes for a strong potential for an attractive return on investment. Michael Maloney makes a great case for why $10,000 gold is the bare minimum of gold's true potential, with his projections reaching $20,000 to $30,000 and higher.

Indeed, gold has tremendous potential and even boasts a better chart than silver dating back to the 1970's. When comparing a gold chart and silver chart side by side, it's clear that silver may have greater volatility, but over the long-term, silver's price chart is floundering, whereas gold's chart shows a steady uphill climb for over 40 years. Except for a significant dip in the late 1990's and early 2000's, and a recent correction since 2012-2013, gold's performance has been stronger than silver.

Many precious metals investors want to have both silver and gold as they see that each has its own unique properties and potential. The main thing that stops some investors from buying gold is the steep price. While in the late 1990's and early 2000's you could buy an ounce of gold for around $250 to $300, the price has been over $1,000 for about a decade now and that's too steep for many investors. Even many wealthy investors have trouble justifying shelling out over $1,000 for an ounce of gold, especially if they picked up cheaper ounces over the years. Fortunately with gold being offered in fractions of an ounce, such as the 1/10 ounce gold eagle, it's likely that investors can afford at least *some* gold.

Many see gold as being a safer investment than silver. It's certainly less volatile, and the price of gold has shown tremendous strength in retaining its value over many centuries. Though both metals have their strengths and weaknesses, silver is more the "jackpot lottery ticket" while gold is the "safe haven" investment. If you can afford to buy some of each, you'll be diversified and able to reap the rewards of owning both when the metals finally find their fair market values.

When?

When will silver find its fair market value? Quite simply, no one knows. There were people in 1980 who were *certain* silver would continue to rise, but it did not. Silver fell and languished for several years. It could be argued that things are different today than they were then, and that's true, yet there were people in 2011 who were *certain* silver would continue to rise, and yet it did not. With the price of silver being intentionally and artificially suppressed, it's anyone's guess as to when the price suppression will end, or if silver will take off in spite of it. One thing is certain, and that's the fact that the price of silver cannot be held back forever. Eventually the price of silver will begin to reflect its true value as the metal seeks fair market value.

If the United States Geological survey is correct in their estimates and massive silver shortages begin to become evident within the next 10-15 years, it's likely the price of silver will begin a strong rise in that period of time or sooner.

The fact remains that silver is a not only money, not only a valuable commodity, but it's also a natural resource that is not renewable and exists both in the ground and above ground in finite quantities. As long as the human race continues to inhabit the Earth and as long as the industrial demands remains high, silver will continue to be consumed, used, burned up, and will become increasingly more rare. As silver becomes more rare, and as the need for silver continues to grow, the laws of supply and demand will eventually cause the price of silver to rise. Never in history has silver been less loved than it is right now. All the factors and centuries of history have lined up just right to make silver quite possibly the greatest investment opportunity of the century. One day silver will find its fair market value. Maybe not today and not tomorrow, but one day it will happen. When it does, will you be there to benefit from this rare opportunity?

What Then?

What's happening with silver right now is unprecedented. Never before has a widely used and needed resource been on the verge of possible extinction. There's no telling how the rise in silver will eventually play out, but one thing is practically inevitable, and that's silver finding its fair market value. The price can't be suppressed forever—eventually the general public will wake up. As silver becomes more scarce and industrial demand increases, silver prices will rise. If silver becomes rare enough, industry might be forced to use other metals that may not work quite as well and may currently be more costly. Like gold. Gold is more costly at present, but whether it will be in the future, no one can say. In the future, if silver becomes too expensive, gold may be needed to replace silver wherever it is possible to do so. Perhaps other technological advances will take place and industry will find a way to thrive without silver, but that is doubtful.

One possible outcome, though unlikely, is that vast silver deposits are discovered within the Earth's crust, enabling silver to remain at more reasonable prices. Should this occur, economic upheaval and/or a currency crisis could still send the precious metal skyrocketing. Once a more sound currency is established (a global currency is one possibility), precious metals prices may return to more affordable levels. If silver rises because of a currency crisis and *not* the general scarcity of the metal, there will likely be a "best time" to sell—when the price of the metal peaks, then once the economy or the currency crisis has stabilized, silver may return to more normal levels. This is a perfect example of what Michael Maloney refers to as "wealth cycles."By jumping ship as one investment peaks and moving into another undervalued investment opportunity, adept investors can continue to profit in any market and at any time.

In the event that silver prices begin to rise because of extreme scarcity of the metal, there may ultimately be no peak. For a limited resource with growing demand and dwindling supply, who can say how high the price will go? One way or another, the future of silver looks exciting and precious metals investors stand to create abundant wealth for themselves as long as they are able to prepare for what's coming our way.

What Now?

What should we do in the meantime? This is the time to prepare. This is the time to study, to learn about the history of currency and precious metals so that we can better understand what's coming in the future. This is the time to save up currency while it still has some (perceived) value and to use that currency to buy precious metals, to acquire real money, sound money: silver and gold. When silver is unloved, undervalued, beaten down, and all but forgotten—this is the time to set aside whatever currency you can spare and just keep stacking that silver.

Escape Plan

In one of the James Bond movies, Q tells James that he's always tried to teach him two things: "Never let them see you bleed, and always have an escape plan." As an investor, you must have an escape plan. Successful stock and commodities traders know at what price they'll sell before they even enter a trade. They set a price target on the upside, and a stop-loss should the trade go against them. When buying precious metals, smart investors must have an ideal price target on the upside for which they plan to sell, and also a stop-loss price should the price of their investments begin to tank. The good news for silver investors is that prices aren't likely to go much lower from here. We're at, or near the bottom for silver right now at $15.

Successful investors are also adept at calculating the risk versus the potential reward. The spot price of silver is $15.27 at the moment, and the lowest silver has been in the past nine years was $13.89. The price of silver has dropped to the $14 area a few times in the past few years, where it found strong support and then began to rise once more. There is strong support around the $14 level, meaning a drop below that level is possible, but unlikely. The lower silver drops, the more eager long-term investors will purchase. Investors who are not in silver for the long run may want to set a stop loss somewhere below $14 if they're not willing to take on much risk. Even if the unexpected happens and silver continues to drop to new multi-year lows, the silver price will drop, then bounce, drop, then bounce. For any investors to get out of silver and walk away should the price continue to fall, it's best to sell on a bounce if they can be patient and wait.

Silver tends to hold its value over the years, so the downside risk is minimal, while the upside potential is practically unlimited. If an investor chooses to sell all his or her silver if the price drops to $13, their risk is about $2 per ounce. Since silver has already reached $49 twice, it's feasible it will reach that price again, meaning the potential reward is at least $34 per ounce. Therefore the risk/reward ratio is 1:17. Any wise investor knows this is one of the best risk/reward ratios to be found.

The risk/reward ratio is quite attractive, but precious metals investment is not a get rich quick scheme. It takes time and patience, as the metals tend to move slow. Investors who do not want to stay in the game long-term should devise an escape plan if they grow tired of waiting. An effective escape plan should illustrate when, where, and how you will get out should the investment turn against you or you grow tired of waiting. The good news is that once you begin to buy silver or gold, you don't have to be committed to it for life. You can sell and get out at any time. Silver and gold are extremely liquid, meaning there are many places you can sell, and those places will often buy however much you're looking to unload. From coin shops, to pawn shops, to eBay, there's no shortage of places that will be eager to buy your gold and silver. You may want to have a *Plan A* and a *Plan B* for when and where you will sell if you decide to get out. You'll also want to know what percentage of the melt value each place pays so you can be sure you're getting the most cash for your precious metals when you sell. Also know how each place pays. Some places truly give cash for silver and gold, while other places will simply cut a check. An escape plan helps minimize risk, and with any investment, investors needs to protect themselves.

Having a good escape plan will not only protect an investor from risk, it will also help ensure maximum profits on the upside for those looking to stay in the game long-term. However, for anyone who decides precious metals investment is not for them, they are free to get out at any time. The great news is that when things begin to heat up again in the precious metals markets, an investor can always buy back in whenever they so choose. In the meantime, price fluctuations will vary, but rest assured silver will one day find its fair market value. When it does, will you be there to reap the rewards?

Selected Bibliography

1. Barisheff, Nick- *$10,000 Gold: Why Gold's Inevitable Rise Is the Investor's Safe Haven.* John Wiley & Sons Canada, Ltd., 2013.

2. Lewis, Nathan- *Gold: The Once and Future Money* John Wiley & Sons, Inc., 2007.

3. Maloney, Michael- *Guide to Investing in Gold & Silver.* Business Plus, Hachette Book Group, 2008.

4. Marcus, Chris- *The Big Silver Short: How The Wall Street Banks Have Left The Silver Market In Place For The Short-Squeeze Of A Lifetime.* Independently published, 2020.

5. Oakes, Robert- *Coins:The Beginning Collector.* Mallard Press, 1992.

6. Yeoman, R.S.- *A Guide Book of United States Coins (The Official Red Book).* Whitman Publishing, LLC., 2011.

Notes

[1] Oakes, Robert- *Coins:The Beginning Collector*. Mallard Press, 1992.
[2] Oakes, Robert- *Coins:The Beginning Collector*. Mallard Press, 1992.
[3] Oakes, Robert- *Coins:The Beginning Collector*. Mallard Press, 1992.
[4] https://www.usinflationcalculator.com/
[5] https://pubs.usgs.gov/fs/2006/3097/fs2006-3097.pdf
[6] https://www.silverinstitute.org/silver-supply-demand/
[7] https://www.wealthdaily.com/articles/silver-is-now-rarer-than-gold/85935
[8] https://www.usgs.gov/centers/nmic/silver-statistics-and-information
[9] https://www.marketreview.com/silver/market/
[10] https://www.commoditytrademantra.com/tag/silver-short-positions/
[11] https://www.kitco.com/news/2020-04-28/CPM-Group-pandemic-to-dent-silver-supply-and-demand-in-2020.html
[12] https://www.historylearningsite.co.uk/modern-world-history-1918-to-1980/weimar-germany/hyperinflation-and-weimar-germany/
[13] http://cointrackers.com/coins/334/1889-cc-morgan-silver-dollar/

Printed in Great Britain
by Amazon

45122511R00059